SIGH AND SERENADE

VERSES OF LOVE AND LONGING

SAMPRITI BORAH

To my family, my parents,

Who saw meaning in the gibberish of my childhood notebooks,

Who understood my words before they had form or clarity,

And who believed in me even when I was still finding my voice.

Contents

Preface

Dear Readers,

Welcome to Sigh and Serenade: Verses of Love and Longing. This collection is born from sudden thoughts and inspirations, capturing fleeting moments when feelings and ideas emerged from the depths of my heart and mind. As Tagore beautifully writes, "I seem to have loved you in numberless forms, numberless times... in life after life, in age after age, forever." These poems are reflections of that eternal love—the kind that stretches beyond time and space, weaving through lifetimes and generations.

Dearest begins with vivid images and heartfelt emotions, painting a love that is boundless and beyond the ordinary. My Love speaks of a deep affection, as vast as the endless ocean, and as constant as a guiding star. Endless explores the timeless nature of true love, promising a bond that lasts even beyond life and death.

Through these verses, I hope to capture the universal experience of love and longing, inviting you to find echoes of your own feelings within them. These words are meant to bring comfort, inspiration, and a deep sense of connection to the endless ways in which love endures.

May these poems speak to your heart as they have to mine.

With gratitude,

Sampriti Borah

1. Dearest

A red moon on the edge of the open sky
and an empty hut in the middle of the open field
Just like you and me
There are many dreams of you and me and,
There is a huge sky in the middle.
I'm not going to lost into the blue of the sky like a poetic lover,
Only the blackness of the sky is special to me,
That you are in there.
A lotus flower in the middle of the tired river
And on the shore I am , a sailor without a rudder,
There is a red river between you and me.
The rose bush is nearby
But I didn't love roses and never will.

2. A love song of mine

Drenched in your showers of love,
My desert..
You are like an endless love poem
I'm a tiny piece of blank paper...
Oh dearest,
How can I keep your enormous bosom,
In my inexperienced arms?
As the morning rays
cast light on the dark sky ,
Your presence takes my gloom away.
You are like the empyrean,
I am only a subtle star of it.
You, a melodious song to me
I am the echo of it.
Oh dearest, how can I keep your infinite love,
Bound in my tiny heart.

3. The Passionate

Only I have the right to be near,
To hold your gaze, to quell your fear.
In the hush of dawn, where whispers stray,
I'll guard your heart.

No shadow, no echo, no hue,
Shall dare to linger closer than I do.
For in your warmth, my world ignites,
Only I shall relish in your sacred light.

Through storms that roar, through skies that weep,
This bond we share runs strong and deep.
So let the world with envy see—
Only I hold the right to be close to thee.

4. Bliss

Under the blissful night's arms,
Where stars adorn the sky,
A cool breeze whispers through the air,
In summer's this warmth, beyond compare.

In my heart nature cast their spell,
And in the distance,
A bird's song soothes away all pain.

This tranquil scene, a symphony,
Of peace and beauty, wild and free,
In harmony with Earth's sweet song,
I find my soul where I belong.

5. Thirst

In a forest of towering trees, I wander,
Grass underfoot, sunlight streaming yonder.
Thirsty and weary, I seek solace near,
Drawn by the distant waterfall's clear.

Following the deer and its fawn,
Towards the source, we journey on.
At the waterfall, a scene unfolds,
With butterflies dancing, nature's stories told.

As the deer drinks from the waterfall
I find my thirst quenched in this tranquil space.
No need for water, the moment is complete,
In nature's sanctuary, I find peace.

6. Echoes of downpour

Outside, the rain pours down,
The earthy scent fills the air around.
A rainbow peeks behind the mango tree,
As raindrops fall on mangoes, tempting to see.
Birds seek shelter from the rain,
Underneath the mango tree, they remain.

In the midst of the downpour's song,
Nature's melody plays all day long.
The rhythmic patter of raindrops, so sweet,
Creates a soothing, calming beat.

The earth drinks in the rain's embrace,
Each drop a kiss upon its face.
Mangoes glisten with every drop that falls,
As if nature's tears, each one recalls.

The birds, they chatter, cozy and dry,
Taking refuge under the mango tree's sky.
Their colorful feathers shine with each hue,
As the rainbow above blends red, green, and blue.

In this moment, nature finds its peace,
As rain and rainbow coexist with ease.
And though the storm may rage and pour,
There's beauty to be found, of that, we can be sure.

7. My love

My love is for you like a ocean vast,deep..
With no end in sight.
You are my universe, my guiding star.
In cool breezy air i can hear only you.

Your voice,a melody in day and night,
Filling my soul with pure delight.
In the air ,a scent , sweet.
Not stargazers but your percept.

Stronger than any fragrance
Is your scent, my love!
In every breath i find your essence,
You're cherish forever in my heart.

8. Endless

In the depths of time, you exist,
Through past and present, you persist.
Into eternity, you'll endure,
Beyond life and death, that's for sure.

You are mine, my love so true,
To the brink of insanity, I'll pursue.
In this endless dance, we're intertwined,
Forever together, our souls combined.

9. Desires unveiled

In the quiet whispers of the day,
Where dreams and hopes find their way,
I await the moment, when our souls entwine,
And in your eyes, my world aligns.

In your gaze, all my desires repose,
I excel at your touch,
With every heartbeat, I long to see
The day when you and I are be reunite.

Let destiny weave its intricate thread,
For in your arms, my fears are shed.
All desires find their end, it's true,
When I finally meet you, and our love is anew.

10. A Love's Reverie

In winter's grasp, memories come to call,
A season wrapped in blankets of the past.
Within its chill, your absence does enthrall,
And every day, your memory does last.

I long to hear your voice, to see your face,
As winter's cold evokes our cherished days.
In reverie, your love I still embrace,
Each memory a light through shadowed haze.

Though miles apart, our hearts still beat as one,
In winter's grasp, our love forever true.
Through memories, our journey's just begun,
And in my heart, I'll always be with you.

11. Unseen Flames

In the quiet depths where shadows softly play,
Your words echo, though I seem not to hear,
Your passion, determination, and love—
Veiled in the mist of time, unseen by me.

Yet, in the silence, a whisper stirs,
A gentle plea that reaches through the void,
To touch the heart that yearns to understand,
To feel the fire that burns within your soul.

Forgive me, beloved, for I am blind,
To the depths of your passion, hidden well,
But now I see, with eyes wide open wide,
The love, the determination, the fire inside.

12. Echoes of Affection

In the quiet corners of your mind, I dwell,
A whisper in the shadows, longing for your gaze,
If you remember me, relief floods my soul,
But without your touch, I shatter like glass.

My love, deep-rooted, from the depths of my heart,
An unending river, flowing endlessly,
No matter how you turn, how you try to ignore,
I'll walk beside you, in every path you tread.

13. The fire within

In the quiet moments, when memories stir,
The old times visit us once more,
A gentle whisper from the past,
A reminder of the love we shared.

Within our hearts, a fire burns,
A flame that refuses to be quenched,
Its warmth, a comfort in the darkest nights,
Its light, guiding us through the shadows.

In the depths of our being, it resides,
A fire that courses through our veins,
In the form of blood, it flows,
Its red hue, a symbol of our love.

Through the trials and tribulations,
Through the highs and lows,
This fire remains, unwavering,
A testament to the strength of our bond.

14. Streams of serenity

In the corner of my chest, a hibiscus blooms,
Its vibrant petals reaching for the light,
While in the opposite corner, a fire consumes,
Casting shadows in the dimness of the night.

Within the closed room of my blind mind,
A picture forms, faint yet clear to see,
My heart, an inhabited space, confined,
A landscape where you flow, wild and free.

Like a gentle stream, you ease the fire's ire,
The hibiscus thrives, revived by your grace,
In this chest of mine, where passions aspire,
You bring calm to the chaos, a soothing embrace.

15. The golden tree

In a bright starry night i was awake
to your breath.
Sometimes, my heart was stunned by the web of your words.
Like a caged bird, I am limited to you.
There was a golden tree in my heart,
And now,now my nights are full of horrors.
The web of word just trangled me,
The wild creeper killed the golden tree.
I can't decide the bird was free or dead,
A deep breath breaks the silence around.

16. Love's Doom

In moments, truth stood firm, a guiding light,
And God's presence, in shadows, softly shone.
Affection bloomed, a sweet and tender sight,
Love, our worship, a bond we called our own.

Yet, madness crept, staining our sacred bond,
Tainting love's purity with its dark gloom.
In its wake, affection and truth, beyond,
Love, once revered, now bowed to its doom.

17. Colours concealed

Underneath my ribs, a tree blooms eternally,
Silent flowers, scentless yet ever-present.
When you find him, convey this truth:
I have a message meant only for him.

For seasons uncounted, I've hidden my colors,
Shades of dawn, twilight, and the spaces in between.
My longing grows as time cycles,
Each petal a secret, each leaf a silent plea.

Tell him that my heart holds a garden,
Vibrant with unspoken words and unseen shades.
In every season, my soul reaches out,
Hoping he'll understand the silence of my blooming tree.

18. Elysium's Voyage

I could recount a thousand reasons why
To fall for you, but let that be unsaid.
If I began, it would take countless years,
And time is not a luxury we have.
Just let me touch you with the deepest love.

Listen, my dear, your eyes are like the sea,
An endless, vast expanse where I would sail.
Your eyes are like the boundless sky above,
In which I long to soar with wings of dreams.
Accept my love, my dear, for all of time.

For in your gaze, I find my world anew,
A universe where love is infinite.
Let's cast away the needless words and doubts,
And live within the silence of our hearts.
Together, we'll embrace eternity.

19. Seasons of solitude

In the depth of my mind, depression lingers,
Yet you, a beacon of hope, await,
With promises of new beginnings, brighter days.

I wonder, will you hold onto the promises made,
Or let them fade, like memories lost
In the radiant smile of a passing woman?

One by one, the six seasons sang the song
Of your absence, leaving me longing.
Do you find solace in verse? like me..
Will you share the ache of your heart with me?

For me, a blank page and pen are the sole means
To converse with you, there is no other way.

20. Secret pierce

In the depths of my gaze, a flame alights bright,
Yet veiled by silence, it burns through the night.
Unseen by all, my fervor takes flight,
Within, I wrestle, in shadows of plight.

Invisible to eyes, this fire's embrace,
My soul whispers secrets, in silent grace.
Unknown, the depths of my internal space,
Danionin's sting, a haunting trace.

So I journey on, through the unseen fire's glow,
A silent struggle, none but I know.
Invisible wounds, within me they grow,
Yet onward I tread, through the depths below.

21. Between sand and death

You have a truth, and I have one,
A shadow cast beneath the sun.
A lie has guided your gaze,
Through fleeting nights and days.

Life slips softly, like sand through hand,
A fragile wisp, a fleeting strand.
And death, it waits, with silent tune,
A patient guest, for only us.

What truth, what lie, can bridge the divide?
What path remains, what will abide?
For all that's real may fade away,
Yet in its loss, truths find their way.

22. Fragments of life

In the garden of memories, flowers bloom,
Reviving tales of joy and gloom.
Thorns pierce, causing pain untold,
In love's embrace, and hate's stronghold.

My love, a madness, knows no bound,
My hatred, a poison, all around.
An incomplete tale, waiting to be told,
A story's end, yet to unfold.

The chapter where I'll meet my fate,
A journey paused, a lingering wait.
In life's intricate, mysterious plot,
The final page, not yet caught.

www.ingramcontent.com/pod-product-compliance
Lightning Source LLC
Chambersburg PA
CBHW030510170726
47990CB00008BA/3137